HARK

Hark

DAILY DEVOTIONS FOR CHRISTMAS FROM "HARK THE HERALD ANGELS SING"

Gwendolyn Harmon

Learning Ladyhood Press

Copyright © 2020 by Gwendolyn Harmon

All rights reserved. No part of this book may be reproduced in any manner whatsoever without written permission except in the case of brief quotations embodied in critical articles and reviews.

First Printing, 2020

All Scripture is from the King James Version

Cover photos by Sherrilyn Shaw, used by permission.

To *you*, dear reader.
May your Christmas be blessed with the
joy, peace, and hope
of a heart near to the Savior.

Contents

Preface		1
1	Heralding Angels	5
2	Glory to the Newborn King	7
3	Peace on Earth	9
4	Mercy Mild	11
5	Reconciled	13
6	Joyful Nations	15
7	Proclaim it!	17
8	Heavenly Adoration	19
9	Everlasting	21
10	Late?	23
11	Virgin-Born	25
12	Veiled	27
13	God Incarnate	29
14	Pleased	31
15	My Immanuel	33
16	Heaven-Born	35
17	Prince of Peace	37

18	Sun of Righteousness	39
19	Light and Life	41
20	Risen to Heal	43
21	Laying Glory Aside	45
22	To Die No More	47
23	Raised with Him	49
24	Second Birth	51
25	Glory	53

Preface

Hark is a word we hardly ever hear nowadays. It is a call to stop and hear, to listen. During the busy days of the Christmas season, it can be difficult to find time to simply stop and listen to all the glorious truths we are celebrating. And yet, in this season, we may be reminded of those same truths everywhere we turn, if only we will stop long enough to really listen.

The words to the song, "Hark, the Herald Angels Sing" were written by Charles Wesley, and contain many precious truths about Christ's birth, life, and the purpose of His coming: all the things Christmas is meant to celebrate. Each day, there is a short reading designed to draw your heart and mind to a particular aspect of Christ's birth. It is my prayer that these will help you to go about each day with a heart full of wonder and worship as you celebrate the Savior's birth.

Hark, the Herald Angels Sing

Hark, the herald angels sing,
"Glory to the newborn King;
Peace on earth, and mercy mild,
God and sinners reconciled!"
Joyful all ye nations rise,
Join the triumph of the skies;
With th'angelic hosts proclaim,
"Christ is born in Bethlehem!"

Hark, the herald angels sing,
"Glory to the newborn King."

~

Christ, by highest heaven adored;
Christ, the Everlasting Lord!
Late in time, behold Him come
Offspring of the Virgin's womb.
Veiled in flesh the Godhead see;
Hail, th'incarnate Deity,
Pleased as man with men to dwell,
Jesus, our Emmanuel.

Hark, the herald angels sing,
"Glory to the newborn King."

~

Hail, the heaven-born Prince of Peace,
Hail, the Sun of Righteousness!
Light and life to all He brings,
Risen with healing in His wings.
Mild, He lays His glory by,
Born that man no more may die,
Born to raise the sons of earth,
Born to give them second birth.

Hark, the herald angels sing,
"Glory to the newborn King."

~Charles Wesley~

1

Heralding Angels

Hark, the herald angels sing

A herald is one who announces. In Medieval times, a herald would have been a military officer serving as an ambassador, carrying messages between the king or nobleman he served and another leader. Heralds would also bring news, proclaiming it to others as an official spokesman.

Hebrews tells us that the angels are God's servants, or ministering spirits. Despite the emphasis on angels throughout this season, the truth is that they are only the messengers; the heralds of God, proclaiming His words to us. Wherever angels appear in the Christmas narrative, they appear with messages from God.

The "herald angels" in our hymn text are the angels which appeared to the shepherds, bringing them the news that the promised Savior had at last arrived. They technically did not "sing" their song: the Bible merely says that they praised God, *saying* the words.

But regardless of whether the words were sung or spoken, the message is still the same. The Savior *has* come, and He can *still* be found by those who seek Him. It is the most joyful message ever carried in the history of heraldry: *"For unto you is born this day in the city of David a Savior, which is Christ the Lord." (Luke 2:11)*

Take time to consider: what does the coming of the Savior mean for you?

2

Glory to the Newborn King

Hark, the herald angels sing,
"Glory to the newborn King"

As the angelic herald delivered the news of the long-awaited Savior, it was as if all heaven was filled to bursting with the joy of the message, and a multitude of angels suddenly appeared, saying, *"Glory to God in the highest, and on earth peace, good will toward men."*

The angels were not to be recipients of the salvation which the newborn King would purchase. They had no sins to be forgiven. They were in no need of reconciliation with God. They would not partake in the glorious substitution of Christ's righteousness for mankind's sin, and yet the message still moved them to glorify God in verbal exclamation of praise.

You and I have much more reason to rejoice in the message of the Savior's birth. We not only rejoice that the Savior came; we live in the reality that the Savior came for *us*. Christmas for the Christian is not just the commemoration of a historic event, but the celebration of a continuing reality. We live in the afterglow of the glory that is the coming of Christ to earth to die for our sins. That is why we of all people should be filled with joy during the Christmas season.

And, like the angels, that joy should fill us to bursting with words of praise with which we glorify God to those around us, speaking constantly of the glorious reason for the Christmas season: our own salvation, as well as salvation to any and all who would receive it.

Does the thought of Christ's gift of salvation fill you with joy?

3

Peace on Earth

Peace on earth and mercy mild

Have you ever noticed that no matter how much the world seeks peace, it never seems to find it? The truth is, apart from God, there is no peace. If we want peace on earth, we must look to the newborn King who gave Himself so that we might have peace with God.

The joy of salvation carries with it the peace of knowing that our sin has been forgiven. We do not have to wonder if we have done enough good to merit heaven: in God's sight, *"all our righteousnesses are as filthy rags." (Isaiah 64:6)*

The security of our salvation is rooted in the fact that *Christ* has done the saving work; we simply received it by faith. As Ephesians 2:8-9 says,

"For by grace are ye saved through faith; and that not of yourselves: it is the gift of God: Not of works lest any man should boast."

The peace of Christmas is like its joy: it is not something we can somehow work up in ourselves. The peace and joy of Christmas well up inside us as a response to the truth of what Christmas means *personally* to you and to me.

Are you basking in the peace of knowing Christ has paid for your sin once and for all?

4

Mercy Mild

Peace on earth and mercy mild

Joy and peace are both words we hear often this time of year, but mercy is not so common. This might be because the world has a counterfeit of joy and peace. It has crafted its own private interpretation of the meaning of those words, but *mercy* has been more difficult to redefine. It is a word that encapsulates the significance of Christ's birth.

The angels came bearing a message of mercy. We had earned our punishment, *"For the wages of sin is death,"* but God mercifully intervened: *"the gift of God is eternal life through Jesus Christ our Lord." (Romans 6:23)* The glories and wonders of Christmas all find their root in the mercy of God.

And it's not just any mercy: the mercy of God is *mild.* When Charles Wesley penned these words, *mild* would have meant gentle, kind, compassionate, even tender. Perhaps he was thinking of the words of Zachariah in Luke 1:77-79:

"To give knowledge of salvation unto His people by the remission of their sins, Through the tender mercy of our God; whereby the Dayspring from on high hath visited us, To give light to them that sit in darkness and in the shadow of death, to guide our feet into the way of peace."

Christmas is a time to remember the tender mercy of God, that looked upon us in the filthiness of our sin and had compassion on us, providing a way for us to be clean.

What does it mean for you that God's mercy is mild?

5

Reconciled

God and sinners reconciled.

Sin is the great separator. It comes between us and the holy God whose perfect righteousness must by necessity remain wholly separate from sin. But when Jesus Christ came to earth, He left the holy, perfect, sin-free throne room of God to dwell among a race who were literally born with sin in their hearts.

Listen to these truths from Colossians: *"For it pleased the Father that in Him [Christ] should all fulness dwell; And, having made peace through the blood of His cross, by Him to reconcile all things unto Himself; by Him, I say, whether they be things in earth, or things in heaven. And you, that were sometime alienated and enemies in your mind by wicked works, yet now hath He reconciled in the body of His flesh through death, to present you holy and unblameable and unreproveable in His sight" (1:19-22)*

You see, *we* have been reconciled to *God*, not the other way around. The coming of Christ was not God descending to our sinfulness, but rather God reaching down to lift us up to His righteousness.

2 Corinthians 5:21 says, *"For He hath made Him to be sin for us, who knew no sin; that we might be made the righteousness of God in Him."* Reconciliation comes as we exchange our sin for Christ's righteousness.

How will the truth of reconciliation affect your life today?

6

Joyful Nations

Joyful, all ye nations rise
Join the triumph of the skies

Reconciliation is wonderful, but we must remember that it's not just for you and me. 2 Peter 3:9 reminds us that God is *"not willing that any should perish, but that all should come to repentance."* When Jesus paid the price for our sin on the cross, He also paid the price for the whole world, *"That whosoever believeth on Him should not perish, but have everlasting life." (John 3:16)*

Jesus' final command to His disciples (and by extension, to us) was *"Go ye into all the world, and preach the gospel to every creature." (Mark 16:15)*

It is our responsibility to share the message of reconciliation with all nations, just as someone shared that message with us. 2 Corinthians 5:18 says that God, having first reconciled us to Himself, *"hath given to us the ministry of reconciliation."*

Perhaps you aren't sure how to share the gospel in another country. After all, most of us have not been called to be a foreign missionary. We have all, however, been called to be part of that great commission, whether through giving, praying, going, or all three.

How is the Holy Spirit burdening you to spread the gospel to the nations?

7

Proclaim it!

With th'angelic host proclaim
Christ is born in Bethlehem!

As we have seen, the angels were not the only messengers sent to proclaim the good news of the Savior. You and I also were meant to proclaim it, and Christmas is a season full of opportunities to proclaim.

When our hearts full of the joy and peace of our own reconciliation with God, we will naturally begin proclaiming it to the world, or, at least, to everyone we meet.

Our world needs to hear about the newborn King, who came to earth to live a sinless life and give Himself to pay for our sin. They need to know that He alone is *"the way, the truth and the life"* and that the only way to be reconciled with God is through Him. *(John 14:6)* They need to hear about the Christ who was born in Bethlehem.

The joy and peace of Christmas has always been meant to be shared. That is why we gather with family and friends to celebrate. But for the unsaved, the joy and peace are superficial. It is just the outward shell of hyped-up happiness without true joy or peace at its center. They need to hear about the Savior whose birth they are ignorantly and meaninglessly celebrating.

Whom does God want you to share the message of Christmas with today?

8

Heavenly Adoration

Christ, by highest heaven adored

Have you ever thought about what Christ left when He came to earth? In heaven, everything was pure, holy, perfect, and glorious. He was worshipped day and night by angelic beings. There was no end to their adoration, and He was never denied, even for the smallest instant, the glory and honor which were and are His due.

And yet, He left all that to come to earth. You may have noticed, it's not perfect here. It isn't pure or holy, and it isn't glorious. There is pain, sickness, and death. Things decay. Things break. People sin.

Jesus Himself was often misunderstood or persecuted. Very rarely was He shown any honor, and apart from the Mount of Transfiguration, His form was not at all glorious. In fact, Isaiah 53 says that, *"He hath no form or comeliness; and when we shall see Him, there is no beauty that we should desire Him." (53:2)*

The few accounts of Christ's heavenly appearance describe Him as radiating glory, so that He glows like a flame. In heaven, God the Son visibly displays God's glory. As God, He wields all authority and power. In heaven, what He says is instantly done. Yet in His tender mercy and love, He *"made Himself of no reputation, and took upon Him the form of a servant, and was made in the likeness of men: And being found in fashion as a man, He humbled Himself, and became obedient unto death, even the death of the cross." (Philippians 2:7-8)*

And He did all that to rescue *you.*

Which of the things Jesus left to come to earth touches your heart the most?

9

Everlasting

Christ, the Everlasting Lord

Christmas is the celebration of Christ's birth, but His birth was not His beginning. John 1 tells us that *"In the beginning was the Word, and the Word was with God, and the Word was God." (v.1)* A quick look at the following verses of that chapter shows us that the "Word" John is talking about is Jesus Christ. He is God, and as God, He is eternal.

2 Timothy 6:16 describes Jesus as He *"who only hath immortality, dwelling in light which no man can approach unto; whom no man hath seen, nor can see: to whom be honour and power everlasting. Amen."*

So what does God's eternity have to do with us and with Christmas? Well, for one thing, it means that the work of reconciliation Jesus accomplished is also everlasting. Hebrews 9:15 tells us that *"for this cause He is the mediator of the new testament, that by means of death, for the redemption of the transgressions that were under the first testament, they which are called might receive the promise of eternal inheritance."*

2 Thess. 2:16 mentions yet another everlasting benefit of His sacrifice: *"Now our Lord Jesus Christ Himself, and God, even our Father, which hath loved us, and hath given us everlasting consolation and good hope through grace."* Our redemption, our inheritance, our consolation: all that Christ has purchased on our behalf is everlasting. It will never end.

Which of God's everlasting benefits encourage you the most today?

10

Late?

Late in time, behold Him come

When Charles Wesley wrote these words, the word *late* would have had a little different meaning. It could have meant tardy or past time, as we typically use it, but in this context, Wesley would have used the word *late* to mean recently or not long past. In the grand scheme of history, the coming of Christ to earth has indeed happened fairly recently.

Wesley's choice of words may seem to misrepresent God's timing, but it does draw our attention to the long years of waiting endured by generation after generation of Old Testament believers before the promised Savior finally appeared. Of course, from God's perspective, it was *"in due time"* that Christ died. *(Romans 5:6)* But from the human standpoint of those who lived in the centuries before the promised Savior came, it might well have seemed that His coming was "late."

This perspective points out to us the blessing of living in the days after the promise, for we can look back on Christ's coming and payment for sin. No longer do we need the picture of animal sacrifice, which could never cleanse us from sin. *(Hebrews 10:4)* No longer do we need the physical place of God's dwelling, for He has made the way for us each to become a temple of the Holy Spirit.

We look back in faith with grateful hearts on the first coming of Christ, even as we continue the thread of waiting and watching, looking forward to Christ's second coming.

How does the thought of God's perfect timing comfort your heart today?

11

Virgin-Born

Offspring of the virgin's womb

"*Behold, a virgin shall conceive, and bear a Son, and shall call His name Immanuel.*"*(Isaiah 7:14)* This is perhaps one of the most frequently-quoted Old Testament passages dealing with the birth of Christ: In fact, it is one of the prophecies quoted in the book of Matthew as part of the Christmas account. But when was the last time you stopped to think about *why* the virgin birth is so important?

I have to admit, I hadn't thought about it in a while, and when I did, the answer didn't come to mind as quickly as I would have liked. But the virgin birth of Christ is one of the most significant aspects of His coming. Its significance is rooted in the holiness of God.

Jesus was (and is) unique, the *"only begotten Son"* of God Himself. *(John 3:16)* As such, He was uniquely qualified to be our substitute. By coming to earth in a miraculous way, Jesus fulfilled prophecy and laid the foundation for everything we believe Him to be.

Jesus came as *Immanuel*, God with us. He came to be with us, to dwell among us as one of us and yet, as God, He could not be born of man. That would mean inheriting the sin nature passed down from Adam to all humanity. Romans says that through Adam, *"death passed upon all men, for that all have sinned." (Romans 5:12)* The holy God could not be born into sin-ridden flesh. By being born of a virgin, Jesus kept His separateness from sin, while taking His place as one of us.

The miraculous virgin birth of Christ is a key foundation of His sacrifice. Without it, we are only left with an unusually "good" man, who could never have justly satisfied God's wrath on our sin and reconcile us to a holy God.

Which aspect of the virgin birth is most significant to you?

12

Veiled

"Veiled in flesh, the Godhead see"

When Jesus was born, He looked like any other child. Despite the artistic renderings of Jesus with a halo of glory radiating from Him, the Bible is clear that He was just like anyone else. After all, people would have *noticed* a glowing baby. As it was, the only visitors recorded that first night were shepherds.

In Jewish culture of the day, shepherds were the lowest of the low. They were the last people you would invite to see your new baby. But they were the *first* God invited to see His newborn Son.

I have often imagined what baby Jesus would have looked like. Lying in that manger, the shepherds would have found a typical newborn: tiny, precious, wrinkly, and completely ordinary. There would have been no radiant beams of glory from His face: the visible evidences of His Deity were veiled.

But there was one instance when that veil was lifted, just for a little while.

In Matthew 17, we are told that Jesus took Peter, James, and John with Him into a high mountain, and there, Jesus *"was transfigured before them: and His face did shine as the sun, and His raiment was white as the light." (v.2)* His glory was allowed to shine, and Peter, James, and John saw Jesus as He truly was.

John later draws a parallel between Christ's veil and an earthly veil of our own: *"Beloved, now are we the sons of God, and it doth not yet appear what we shall be: but we know that, when He shall appear, we shall be like Him; for we shall see Him as He is." (1 John 3:2)*

There is coming a day when our earthly veil will drop away. We will stand before Christ in our glorified bodies, free from sin, gazing upon Him as He is: no veils between.

What does Christ's veiling of His Deity mean for you?

13

God Incarnate

Hail, th'incarnate Deity

The incarnation is one of the mysteries of Christianity. It is unfathomable. That God Himself would choose to put on flesh, the Creator of the universe choosing to be born as a helpless, fragile baby, is nothing less than amazing. As the Christmas season progresses, we see the nativity scenes, we sing songs like "Away in a Manger", but do we stop to think about the very wonder of God choosing to put on flesh and live among us as a man?

And yet, He did.

The wonder is not just that He *could*, but that He *didn't have to*. He could have chosen to wipe out the entire human race and start fresh with a brand new creation. He could have decided we were not worth saving: because, in a sense, we're not. But instead He chose, not to humble us or to crush us as we rightly deserve, but rather to humble *Himself* and allow *Himself* to be crushed. –And all for *my* sin and *yours*.

That is the significance of the incarnation. God incarnate: in flesh. I love how Philippians 2 describes this: *"Who, being in the form of God, thought it not robbery to be equal with God: but made Himself of no reputation, and took upon Him the form of a servant, and was made in the likeness of men: and being found in fashion as a man, He humbled Himself, and became obedient unto death, even the death of the cross." (vv.6-8)*

The point of the passage is that we, too should have the mind of Christ, to choose to humble ourselves, to obey unto death, to sacrifice ourselves for others. Perhaps the wonder of the incarnation is in part that Christ would allow *us* to reflect the humility and love of His incarnation to those around us.

How is the Holy Spirit prompting you to have "the mind of Christ" in your dealings with others today?

14

Pleased

Pleased as Man with man to dwell

When we think of Christ's earthly life, we think of sacrifice, obedience, and mercy, but was Christ really *pleased* to dwell with us as a man? I think we can find the answer to this question in Psalm 115:3:

"But our God is in the heavens: He hath done whatsoever He hath pleased."

Nothing ever forces God to act. Before He spoke the universe into being, He knew the choices you and I would make each day. He knew that Adam and Eve would choose to sin, and that a substitute would be needed to save mankind from the penalty of their own sin. He also knew that He Himself would be that substitute.

Isaiah 53:10 says of Christ, *"Yet it pleased the Lord to bruise Him."* It's not that God was pleased by Christ's pain, but rather that He was pleased at the fulfilling of His plan of redemption for the people He created and loves.

As a part of the Trinity, Jesus always acts and thinks in perfect unity with the rest of the Godhead. What pleases God the Father pleases God the Son and God the Holy Spirit. The three are in perfect unity. So if the salvation plan of Jesus' birth, life, death, and resurrection pleased the Father, they pleased the Son as well. After all, we were made for His pleasure. *(Revelation 4:11)*

Are you pleased with what pleases God?

15

My Immanuel

Jesus, our Immanuel

Isaiah 9:6 is one of my favorite Christmas passages. You're probably very familiar with it as well:

"For unto us a Child is born, unto us a Son is given: and the government shall be upon His shoulder: and His name shall be called Wonderful, Counsellor, The mighty God, The everlasting Father, The Prince of Peace."

There are many truths packed into this verse, but the one that has stood out to me the most over the years is the phrase *"unto us."*

Christmas can feel like a big celebration of a grand and global event that changed the course of history… and it is. But it is also an individual celebration of the Mighty God, the Everlasting Father, the Prince of Peace, choosing reconciliation and relationship with *me*.

The wonder of the incarnation on a theological scale is real and significant, but on a personal level, it is nothing less than a miraculous display of God's love, not just for the human race as a whole, but also for the individual. It is the celebration that Christ was born, not just for some people out there somewhere, but that He was born *for you*.

And centuries later, He is still *Immanuel*, God with us. Through the indwelling of the Holy Spirit, we have God with us every moment of every day. Christmas is a reminder of the daily reality, both of reconciliation and of relationship.

Are you basking in the personal reality of Immanuel: God with you?

16

Heaven-Born

Hail, the heaven-born Prince of Peace

Have you ever stopped to think that Heaven was well-acquainted with Jesus before He ever lay in that manger? As we have already noted, Jesus is the eternal God, who was present at creation and graced the earth with several pre-incarnate visits that theologians call Theophanies.

Since Jesus had existed in heaven for all of eternity past, and I would guess that the angels had known Him since the first moment of their creation, I have often wondered what they thought of His choice to leave heaven and live on earth as a human.

I Peter 1:12 speaks of the gospel of salvation as something which the angels "desire to look into." I wonder if the inhabitants of heaven watched as Jesus was born, swaddled in rough cloths, and laid in a feeding trough.

Hebrews points out that man was said to have been made *"a little lower than the angels,"* and that, in being born as a man, God Himself chose to be made *lower* than the angels. *"But we see Jesus, who was made a little lower than the angels for the suffering of death, crowned with glory and honour; that He by the grace of God should taste death for every man."* (Hebrews 2:9)

Christ, in a sense, was made lower than the angels when He left heaven, but His return to heaven was in the triumphant glory and honor which is His due as God the Son, who won the victory over death and hell once and for all.

Are you living in the victory Christ won for you?

17

Prince of Peace

Hail the heaven-born Prince of Peace

The title, "Prince of Peace" comes from Isaiah 9:6, which you might remember reading earlier in this book. It bears repeating, however, and will give us some context:

"For unto us a Child is born, unto us a Son is given: and the government shall be upon His shoulder: and His name shall be called Wonderful, Counsellor, The mighty God, The everlasting Father, The Prince of Peace."

There's more to this passage, though: *"Of the increase of His government there shall be no end, upon the throne of David, and upon His kingdom, to order it, and to establish it with judgement and with justice from henceforth even for ever. The zeal of the Lord of Hosts will perform this."* (9:7)

The Baby whose birth we celebrate at Christmas will one day reign for ever and ever. His reign will be supreme and all-encompassing, and it will be built upon the perfect judgement and justice of the all-holy God. His kingdom will be ruled perfectly, and His "golden age" will never have an end.

The joy and wonder of Christmas is not just rooted in the earthly benefits of salvation. Take time to look up, to consider the bright and blessed future that awaits the saved in Christ, and be encouraged by the glory to come.

What encourages you the most about a future with Jesus as your literal King?

18

Sun of Righteousness

Hail, the Sun of Righteousness!

1 John tells us that *"God is light, and in Him is no darkness at all." (1:5)* In the heavenly New Jerusalem, Revelation tells us,

"the city had no need of the sun, neither of the moon, to shine in it: for the glory of God did lighten it, and the Lamb is the light thereof." (21:23)

Here on earth, Jesus is our spiritual source of light. 2 Corinthians 4:6 says, *"For God, who commanded the light to shine out of darkness, hath shined in our hearts, to give the light of the knowledge of the glory of God in the face of Jesus Christ."*

But that light isn't just for us to bask in, although we can and should take time to bask in the light of Christ; it is also for us to *reflect*. Just as the moon reflects the light of the sun, so we are to reflect the light of Christ.

Jesus said, *"Let your light so shine before men that they may see your good works and glorify your Father which is in heaven." (Matthew 5:16)* The way we speak and behave can shine the light of Christ into the lives of those around us, but it can also throw a dark cloud across the light God wants us to shed abroad into the lives of others. It all comes down to obedience.

Christmas can be a challenging time, and it is easy to get busy and stressed and begin yielding to our sinful flesh, instead of to the Holy Spirit. It is crucial that we guard our hearts so that we can keep the light of Christ reflecting off of us that it may fill the lives of others.

How does God want you to reflect Him today?

19

Light and Life

"Light and life to all He brings"

John 1:4 says of Jesus, *"In Him was life; and the life was the light of men."* Jesus came to be the life-giving Light of the world. Listen to what He says about the purpose of His coming to earth:

"I am the light of the world: he that followeth Me shall not walk in darkness, but shall have the light of life."

Before Jesus, we were filled with the darkness of fear and sin, without even a glimmer of hope to brighten our lives. But then, for those of us who have been reconciled through the blood of Christ, there came a day when we experienced the truth of 1 John 1:5 that in God there is no darkness at all. As Isaiah 9:2 prophesies,

"The people that walked in darkness have seen a great light: they that dwell in the land of the shadow of death, upon them hath the light shined."

But Jesus came not just to bring us eternal life, but to fill that life with the light of His presence. Jesus Himself said,

"I am come that they might have life, and that they might have it more abundantly." (John 10:10)

As we walk in the light of His presence, He satisfies us with good things and renews our strength to serve Him. *(Psalm 103:5)*

It is a great privilege to walk in the light. 1 Peter 2:9 is a beautiful summary of this truth.

"But ye are a chosen generation, a royal priesthood, an holy nation, a peculiar people; that ye should shew forth the praises of Him who hath called you out of darkness and into His marvellous light."

We who belong to Christ walk in His light. How absurd it would be for those in the light to stumble around like those in the darkness!

Are you walking in the light of God's presence today?

20

Risen to Heal

Risen with healing in His wings.

This line is an allusion to Malachi 4:1-3, which begins,

"For, behold, the day cometh, that shall burn as an oven; and all the proud, yea, and all that do wickedly, shall be stubble: and the day that cometh shall burn them up, saith the Lord of Hosts, that it shall leave them neither root nor branch." (v.1)

The picture of complete and utter destruction in this first verse is bleak, to be sure, but look at what God says next:

"But unto you that fear My name shall the Sun of righteousness arise with healing in His wings; and ye shall go forth, and grow up as calves of the stall. And ye shall tread down the wicked; for they shall be ashes under the soles of your feet in the day that I shall do this, saith the Lord of Hosts." (v. 4-5)

Although God's hand of judgement would fall, those who feared God's name would be "healed" and be brought out of total destruction to claim total victory over the wicked.

What a picture of the purpose of Christmas! God came to those in utter destruction, bringing healing that would raise them up to be victorious over sin and Satan.

Are you living in victory today?

21

Laying Glory Aside

Mild, He lays His glory by

As we have noted, Charles Wesley would have understood the word *mild* as having a much broader meaning than we do now. To think of Christ laying aside His glory in gentleness or tenderness draws quite a picture to mind.

That is the love of Christ in action: it is Christ, laying aside the rightful vesture of His glorious appearance, and taking instead the lowly, humble, frail form of a human being. This is the picture of God in the flesh, born for you and me.

But His glory was only laid aside for a season. It was to be taken up again after His resurrection, never more to be removed.

However, the glorified body Christ took up retained the scars of His sacrifice: the hands and feet pierced by nails, the side stabbed by a spear. He kept those marks as proof that He had paid the debt of our sin in full.

It is as if Christ took that human body He so tenderly stooped to put on, and upon returning to heaven, laid the mantle of His glory over it; a robe of Deity illuminating the now glorified body of His humanity.

Christ's choice to thus identify Himself with us throughout eternity is another of the wonders of Christmas: that God chose, not just to take, but also to *keep*, the form of man throughout eternity out of His great love for us.

> ***How does Christ's choice to keep the scars of His crucifixion most touch your heart today?***

22

To Die No More

Born that man no more may die

It is so easy to rush past the familiar. If you grew up in or around church, you may have memorized John 3:16 early on in your life, as I did. It has been widely used as a verse to teach children the gospel, and I'm sure it has been rattled off countless times over the years by little children in pursuit of a sticker or a piece of candy.

While I am glad that such a foundational verse is so widely known, I fear that "well-known" often translates into "overlooked". We tend to skim past the verses most familiar to us and look for other "deeper" truths or for something "new" to stand out to us. But there's nothing deeper than the love of God on display in John 3:16, and we would never appreciate the "new" without the foundation of the "old."

So today, take your time. Read through this verse with fresh eyes, considering the love of God that led Him to send Jesus to die, so that we might have eternal life.

"For God so loved the world that He gave His only begotten Son, that whosoever believeth in Him should not perish, but have everlasting life."

What did the Holy Spirit quicken to your heart as you read?

23

Raised with Him

Born to raise the sons of earth

One of the amazing truths of salvation is the fact that we are raised spiritually to a new position in Christ. Ephesians 2 explains,

"And you hath He quickened, who were dead in trespasses and sins; Wherein in time past ye walked according to the course of this world, according to the prince of the power of the air, the spirit that now worketh in the children of disobedience: among whom also we all had our conversation in times past in the lusts of our flesh, fulfilling the desires of the flesh and of the mind; and were by nature the children of wrath, even as others."

That's where you and I started out: wallowing in the mire of our own sin, enslaved to our own wicked desires. We had no way of escaping from our own filthiness. But this passage continues with two of the most glorious words in Scripture:

*"**But God**, who is rich in mercy, for His great love wherewith He loved us, Even when we were dead in sins, hath quickened us together with Christ, (by*

grace ye are saved;) And hath raised us up together, and made us sit together in heavenly places in Christ Jesus" (v.4-6)

Christ truly was "born to raise the sons of earth," to rescue us from the pit of our own depravity and to make us clean, fit to dwell with Him in heaven. In Christ, we have been raised to the place of victory over sin which Christ has already won on our behalf.

This truth carries with it a responsibility: *"If ye then be risen with Christ, seek those things which are above, where Christ sitteth on the right hand of God. Set your affection on things above, not things on the earth." (Colossians 3:1-2)*

Christ has raised you: are you seeking heavenly things?

24

Second Birth

Born to give them second birth

The birth of Christ was a real, literal, human birth. It involved all the pain, discomfort, and challenges of childbirth, and it happened in a real, literal sheltering place for animals. It may have been anything from rough structure to a cave, but animals had been there either way. Christ's birth was, spiritually speaking, enormously significant, but I'm sure at the time it must have seemed just as earthly an experience as could be.

In John 3, Jesus states,

"Verily, verily, I say unto thee, Except a man be born again, he cannot see the kingdom of God." (v.3)

Just as Jesus' literal birth marked His entrance into an earthly family, our "second birth" marks our entrance into the family of God. Galatians 4:4-6 tells us,

"But when the fulness of the time was come, God sent forth His Son, made of a woman, made under the law, To redeem them that were under the law, that we might receive the adoption of sons. And because ye are sons, God hath sent forth the Spirit of adoption into your hearts, crying, Abba, Father."

We celebrate Christ's literal birth, and it is right to do so, but today as you think upon the coming of the Savior, remember that He was born *physically* so that you might be given *spiritual* birth.

How does the truth of your second birth cause your heart to celebrate differently?

25

Glory

Hark the herald angels sing,
Glory to the newborn King

Christmas can be a busy day. Perhaps by the time you pick up this little book and read this page, your Christmas is already well underway. There may be the bustle of cooking and cleaning in preparation for guests, there may be the pitter patter of excited little feet down the hallway early in the morning. There may be presents to open, songs to sing, perhaps even a church service to attend or a long journey to a relative's house.

But somewhere in the busyness of today's Christmas celebrations, I encourage you to carve out some time, even if it's only just a few moments, to sit quietly before God. Harken to the message of the angels, and join with them in their exultant cry:

"Glory to God in the highest, and on earth peace, good will toward men."
(Luke 2:14)

For that truly is what Christmas is all about.

www.ingramcontent.com/pod-product-compliance
Lightning Source LLC
Chambersburg PA
CBHW071035080526
44587CB00015B/2633